Property of
The Public Library of Nashville and Davidson County
225 Polk Ave., Nashville, TN 37203
PRUITT BRANCH LIBRARY

JESSE OWENS

by
William R. Sanford
&
Carl R. Green

CRESTWOOD HOUSE
New York

Maxwell Macmillan Canada
Toronto

Maxwell Macmillan International
New York Oxford Singapore Sydney

Library of Congress Cataloging-in-Publication Data
Sanford, William R. (William Reynolds)
　　Jesse Owens / by William R. Sanford and Carl R. Green. — 1st ed.
　　　p. cm. — (Sports immortals)
　　Includes bibliographical references.
　　Summary: A biography of the noted black track star, whose record-breaking performances in college and in the 1936 Berlin Olympics assured him a place in sports history.
　　ISBN 0-89686-742-0
　　1. Owens, Jesse, 1913–1980—Juvenile literature. 2. Track and field athletes—United States—Biography—Juvenile literature. [1. Owens, Jesse, 1913–1980. 2. Track and field athletes. 3. Afro-Americans—Biography.]
I. Green, Carl R.　II. Title.　III. Series.
GV697.O9S264　　1992
796.42'092—dc20
[B]　　91-27185

Photo Credits
Photos courtesy of The Bettmann Archive.

Copyright © 1992 by Crestwood House, Macmillan Publishing Company

All rights reserved. No part of this book may be reproduced or transmitted in any form or by any means, electronic or mechanical, including photocopying, recording, or by any information storage and retrieval system, without permission in writing from the Publisher.

Macmillan Publishing Company　　　Maxwell Macmillan Canada, Inc.
866 Third Avenue　　　　　　　　　1200 Eglinton Avenue East
New York, NY 10022　　　　　　　　Suite 200
　　　　　　　　　　　　　　　　　Don Mills, Ontario M3C 3N1

CRESTWOOD HOUSE

Macmillan Publishing Company is part of the Maxwell Communication Group of Companies.

Produced by Flying Fish Studio

Printed in the United States of America

First edition

10 9 8 7 6 5 4 3 2 1

Contents

A Day for Breaking Records 5

Growing Up Poor 8

A Better Life in Cleveland 10

Run as if the Track Is on Fire 12

The One-Man Team 15

The Buckeye Bullet 19

The Road to Berlin 22

Olympic Gold 25

New Races to Run 28

Building a New Life 32

The Race Comes to an End 37

Jesse Owens, Track Immortal 39

Glossary 43

More Good Reading about Jesse Owens 45

Jesse Owens Trivia Quiz 46

Index 48

A DAY FOR BREAKING RECORDS

The sun rose warm and bright on May 25, 1935. The Ohio State track team had come to Ann Arbor, Michigan, to compete in the **Big Ten** Conference Championships. Larry Snyder, the team's coach, was not looking forward to the meet. Jesse Owens, his star runner, had wrenched his back playing touch football. Hot packs and rubdowns had helped, but the muscles were still stiff and sore. Snyder feared that Jesse would make the injury worse if he ran.

Jesse had other ideas. He begged for the chance to run in the big meet. Snyder refused, but Jesse kept working on him. At last Snyder gave in. He said Jesse could try the 100-yard dash. "Ease up if you feel any pain," he told his star.

Although his back was sore, Jesse kept his mind on the starter's pistol. When the gun went off, he jumped into a quick lead. Seconds later he led the other runners across the finish line. Today judges stop their watches the instant a runner breaks the tape. In 1935 they waited until the runner's back foot crossed the line. Even so, Jesse's time of 9.4 seconds is still considered exceptional. The crowd roared with delight. The **Buckeye** Bullet had tied the world record for the 100-yard dash.

Jesse Owens, 1932

Jesse Owens (right) *ties the world record for the 100-yard dash.*

With a world record in hand Jesse forgot his sore back. He walked to the long jump pit. At his request a friend placed a marker at the current world record distance. On Jesse's first jump he soared well past the marker. The judges measured and measured again. Then they announced that Jesse had set a new world record of 26 feet, 8¼ inches.

Jesse now owned one record and had tied a second. How could he top that? Jesse answered the challenge by running the 220-yard dash in 20.3 seconds. That broke an 11-year-old world record. Next came the 220-yard low hurdles. Jesse was tired and this was his weakest event—but not on this day. He ran the hurdles in 22.6 seconds, another world record.

At that point someone pointed out that 220 yards is equal to 201 meters. In running the two 220-yard races, Jesse had also broken two metric records. He was given world records in the 200-meter dash and the 200-meter low hurdles.

Jesse was mobbed by teammates and reporters. In less than an hour he had set five world records and tied a sixth. Sports experts now say that May 25, 1935, was the greatest day in track history. Only Jesse's close friends knew how hard he had worked to make that day happen.

 Jesse broke records while he was still in high school. What world records did he set at the National Interscholastic Meet in 1933?

* Answers to all Trivia Quiz questions can be found on pages 46–47.

GROWING UP POOR

James Cleveland Owens was born on September 12, 1913, in Oakville, Alabama. The family called him J. C. Emma and Henry Owens had already buried three of their 13 children. Sickly little J. C. looked as though he might soon be the fourth. The Owens were too poor to give him the medicines he needed.

Henry made his living as a **sharecropper**. At harvesttime the landowner took half of Henry's crops. This paid for the use of the land and for the family's tiny shack. The shack did not have indoor plumbing, running water or electric lights. Wind and rain found their way through the loose boards.

Being poor meant being hungry as well as cold. Emma did her best to feed her large family. She kept a garden and canned what she grew. Once a year Emma and Henry killed a hog and smoked the meat. They saved the ham and bacon for holidays and birthdays.

J. C. seemed to go from one sickness to the next. Each winter he came down with a "devil's cold." A doctor would have told Emma that the "cold" was **pneumonia**. The best Emma could do was to wrap her son in cotton feed sacks. On the coldest days she let him sleep in front of the fire. When J. C. was six he came down with boils. Boils are swollen, infected pockets in the skin. Without money for a doctor Emma did the only thing she knew how to do. While Henry held the screaming boy, she cut out the boils with a red-hot knife.

That was the year J. C. first walked to school with his brothers and sisters. The one-room school was nine miles away. When

A proud Jesse Owens shows off his medals to his mother.

spring came, the children stayed home to help with the planting. They did not return to school until the crops were gathered in the fall.

The Owenses did not think of themselves as poor. Most of the people who lived near Oakville were sharecroppers, too. But J. C. always wished he had better clothes. When neighborhood girls came to visit he ran off and hid. Each Owens child had one good shirt to wear on Sundays. After church the men liked to hold races. A fine runner, Henry won most of the time.

J. C. was proud of his father's running. He told Henry he wanted to be a runner, too. Henry taught his son what he could. Running helped build up J. C.'s weak lungs and gave him a sense of freedom. When he was running, he felt as though he could go anywhere he chose.

J. C.'s life changed for the better when he was nine. One of his sisters had moved to Cleveland, Ohio. She wrote to tell her parents that they should move north, too. "There's money to be made up here," she wrote. Henry did not want to leave the land he knew so well. It was Emma who pushed him into making the move. She wanted a better life for her children.

Henry sold the family's mules to pay for their tickets. At the station J. C. asked, "Where's the train gonna take us?"

"It's gonna take us to a better life," Emma told him.

A Better Life in Cleveland

Cleveland was a strange new world for the Owens family. Emma and Henry found an apartment in the city's east-side **ghetto**. The children did not notice that one window looked out on an alley. For the first time they had a sink with running water. The rooms were lit by electric lights. Outside they walked on paved streets and enjoyed their first sight of Lake Erie.

 The records Jesse Owens set at the 1936 Olympic Games have fallen one by one. How do his times compare with the current Olympic records?

J. C.'s parents were slow to adjust to their new life. Emma often kept the curtains closed when she was home. Henry missed his farm and the work he knew so well. The children made the change more quickly. J. C. played stickball with the children of Polish, Greek, Chinese and Italian parents. They ignored his color; he ignored their accents. For a treat he went to see cowboy films at a nearby theater.

Emma, Henry and the older children took whatever jobs they could find. Emma washed clothes and scrubbed floors for wealthy white women. Henry and the older boys found work in a steel mill. When times were hard, Henry was the first to be laid off. He was blind in one eye and could not keep up.

Each week the family pooled its money. There was enough to buy new clothes and a few pieces of furniture. Food was a big expense. The family ate a diet of potatoes, beans and bread. Meat was a once-a-week treat. J. C. was growing taller, but he was broomstick thin.

J. C. was ten years old when he enrolled at Bolton Elementary School. No one in the crowded school had much time to spare for a shy black farm boy. Despite his age J. C. was placed in the first grade. The principal thought he did not know how to read and write. When the teacher asked his name, he said, "J. C. Owens" in a soft southern drawl. Thinking he had said "Jesse Owens," she wrote it that way. J. C. was afraid to argue with his new teacher and the name stuck. In time even his family called him Jesse.

Jesse soon moved to a second-grade class. He was older and taller than the other second-graders. His legs barely fit under his desk. Many of his classmates were as new to America as Jesse was to the city. At Bolton they were taught to obey and to work hard. Jesse also learned to be polite and to do tasks on time.

Only Henry missed the old way of life. He was barely 40 years old, but hard work had worn him down. Because he could not read or write, many jobs were closed to him. It was Emma and the older boys who brought in the most money. Emma worked for 30 cents an hour as a maid. At Christmas her wages paid for a fine tree with real ornaments.

To help out, Jesse worked after school and on weekends. He found jobs in a shoe repair shop and in a greenhouse. Compared to working in the fields, sweeping floors and shining shoes seemed easy. Jesse liked the job in the greenhouse best. As he tended the tiny plants, he dreamed of a bright future. Someday, he told himself, he'd own a fine house with a big oak tree in the yard.

The move to Cleveland did not end Jesse's bouts with the "devil's cold." The cold northern winters often put him in bed for days at a time. Jesse did not know it, but he was one of the lucky ones. In those days many people died of pneumonia. Thanks to Emma's care and his own toughness, Jesse always bounced back.

RUN AS IF THE TRACK IS ON FIRE

Jesse moved on to Fairmount Junior High School. He was not sure what he was going to do with his life. At Fairmount all that changed. An Irish gym teacher named Charles Riley took Jesse under his wing.

Along with teaching gym classes Riley coached the school track team. In Jesse the wise old coach saw the makings of a great runner. He also knew that many young men and women

Coach Charles Riley played an important role in the life and athletic career of Jesse Owens.

are gifted with natural speed. Turning that gift into gold medals takes years of training.

Riley took Jesse aside one day. "How would you like to be on the track team when you get into high school?" he asked.

Jesse's face lit up. "I would! I would!" he said.

A problem turned up almost at once. Riley's team worked out after school. Jesse, however, had an after-school job. He could not train with the other boys.

Riley did not give up. He told Jesse to show up before school each day. Jesse could not believe that a white man would go to so much trouble to help him. Yet when he arrived at Fairmount each day, Riley was waiting for him. Coach and pupil soon became close friends.

Jesse began to think of himself as a runner. Each morning he stretched, jumped and ran under Riley's sharp eye. Slowly his body gained strength. When he was tired and his lungs hurt, Riley urged him to keep going. Great athletes, Jesse learned, must dig deep to find the courage they need to win. In some of his early races he gave up when he fell behind.

"Don't worry about the other runners," Riley scolded. "You've got to run to beat yourself."

Riley often took Jesse home to eat with his own family. Jesse began to think of his friend and coach as a second father. He called Riley "Pop." In quiet moments Riley talked about values and dreams. "Coach Riley trained me to be a man as well as an athlete," Jesse said later.

In those days most sprinters ran like halfbacks heading for the goal line. Riley thought this hard-driving technique was a waste of energy. He taught Jesse to "float" down the track. "Keep your head firm and straight like a racehorse," he said. "Run as if the track is on fire. Your feet should barely touch the ground."

After a year of training Riley timed Jesse in a 100-yard dash. To his amazement the 15-year-old Jesse ran the distance in 11 seconds. At first Riley thought his stopwatch was wrong. Asked to run again, Jesse repeated his feat.

In 1928 Jesse ran the 100- and 200-yard dashes for Fairmount. In field events he set two world records for junior high students. First he cleared six feet in the high jump. Then he hit 22 feet, 11 3/4 inches in the long jump. The long hours of practice were paying off.

In 1930 the **Great Depression** struck. All at once running seemed like a luxury. Jesse's brothers lost their jobs. Henry was hit by a cab and his leg was broken. Jesse said he would leave school to go to work. His mother said no. She and Jesse's sisters were earning money by working as maids. Emma insisted that her youngest son go on to high school.

The One-Man Team

Jesse enrolled at East Cleveland Technical High School in the fall of 1930. A confident runner, he had dreams of running in the Olympics someday. Coach Riley did not think his star runner was aiming too high. He told Emma that Jesse was certain to win an Olympic gold medal.

East Tech trained its students for work, not college. The boys learned how to run machines and use tools. Only a few of Jesse's teachers guessed that he did not read well. His homeroom teacher tried to help him, but Jesse did not listen. Sports, work and a busy social life filled his days.

Along with his gold medals Jesse was given a tiny oak tree for each of his Olympic victories. What did he do with those four trees?

The one-time farm boy was now a sharp dresser. Emma made sure of that. Still shy and modest in some ways, Jesse did not swagger around the campus like some athletes did. Many girls chased him, but he was true to Ruth Solomon, his junior high sweetheart. He was also true to his first love, running. When other sports cut into his running time, he dropped them.

Jesse had a stroke of luck his first year at East Tech. The school's new track coach had been a football player in college. Unsure of how to coach track, he asked Charles Riley to help him. Riley jumped at the chance to stay in contact with Jesse.

By his junior year, reporters were calling Jesse a one-man team. His best running events were the 100- and 220-yard dashes. When the team needed points, he ran the hurdles and **anchored** the relay team. His best field event was the long jump. In all, Jesse ran 79 races in high school—and won 75 of them. At many meets he scored more than half of his team's points.

Jesse was invited to try out for the 1932 Olympic Games. He traveled to Evanston, Illinois, to compete in the regional trials. He soon found that the other runners were older and stronger. Jesse ran well but lost to Ralph Metcalfe in both dashes. He was also beaten in the long jump. Later that summer some Olympic runners came to Cleveland for a meet. Jesse gained a measure of revenge by winning the 100 and the 220.

 Jesse and Luz Long became good friends during their epic duel in the long jump. Did they ever meet again?

On his return home from Chicago, where he tied the world record in the 100-yard dash, Jesse receives congratulations from Mayor Ray T. Miller.

Success on the track did not mean Jesse's private life was in order. On August 8 Ruth gave birth to his baby. She named the child Gloria and left school to take care of her. Because she was so young, she lived at home. Her father was so angry that he refused to let Jesse see Ruth and the baby.

If Jesse had married in 1932 he might have quit school to go to work. Instead he was free to win new honors. His classmates chose him to head the student council. As captain of the track team he led the way to a national title. In the final meet of the National Interscholastic Meet, Jesse set a world record of 20.7 seconds in the 220-yard dash. In the 100 he tied the world record of 9.4 seconds. Then to cap his big day he sailed 24 feet, $3^{1}/_{6}$ inches in the long jump. That was a world record for high school students.

Cleveland held a victory parade for the team. With his proud parents riding beside him, Jesse waved to cheering crowds. At city hall the mayor made a speech. He said he looked forward to watching Jesse run again—as a college athlete.

Jesse Owens (left) *with Ralph Metcalfe*

Jesse Owens winning the first heat of the 100-meter dash for Ohio State University.

THE BUCKEYE BULLET

Jesse was not a top student, but he was the country's best high school runner. Many colleges wanted him to run for their track teams. Today a young runner with Jesse's talent would not have to pay to go to college. In 1933 that was not the case. Athletes had to earn their way by working on campus.

Offers flooded into Jesse's mailbox. He studied them all, trying to find a college with a top-notch track program. At last he picked Ohio State University. Larry Snyder, the OSU track coach, was a lot like Pop Riley. Snyder even promised to find a job for Jesse's father.

Jesse leaps through the air during the broad jump event of this 1935 college track and field meet.

To pay his way, Jesse was given a job running a freight elevator. The cleaning crews that he carried from floor to floor needed him only once an hour. That left Jesse with plenty of time to study. He needed those hours—and more. Although his coaches steered him to easy classes, his grades were poor. The lack of study in junior high and high school was catching up with him.

Jesse began his first college track season in the spring of 1934. Coach Snyder liked the young man's smooth style, but he also saw some bad habits. Snyder worked with Jesse to relax his upper body and to improve his start. In the long jump Snyder helped his star gain added distance. Jesse learned to pump his arms and legs as he flew through the air.

In his first year Jesse could not run in varsity meets. He practiced with the team but competed only with the freshmen.

That did not stop him from breaking Big Ten records. Jesse set new marks for freshmen in the 100, 220 and the long jump. Then he went home for the summer to pump gas in a filling station.

In 1935 Jesse took his place on the varsity team. In February the team traveled to New York for an indoor meet. For Jesse and the other black runners it was an old, sad story. Many restaurants would not serve them. In New York they had to slip into their hotel rooms via the freight elevator.

The bad treatment did not affect Jesse's running. Instead of fighting back he saved his energy for the track. In New York he beat the famous Ralph Metcalfe for the first time. Still, Jesse did not win all of his races. Swift sprinters like Eulace Peacock sometimes edged him out at the tape.

Back home in Ohio the Buckeye Bullet made more headlines. To attract a crowd for a big meet, Coach Snyder set up a special stunt. Reporters watched as Jesse started a 100-yard dash while running at top speed. When he crossed the finish line the stopwatches showed an amazing time of 8.4 seconds. A crowd of 12,000 turned out for that meet. Jesse pleased the hometown rooters by winning all three of his events.

In May Jesse set his five world records at the Big Ten meet. Afterward Coach Riley drove him home. Riley told Jesse that his life would never be the same. "From now on," he said, "runners will work extra hard to beat you. The public will pester you. Sportswriters will watch your every move."

Jesse thought about Riley's advice when he went home that summer. It was time to resolve his problem with Ruth's parents. In July her father at last agreed to let Jesse and Ruth get married. Now Jesse felt more at peace. His poor grades did not worry him. His thoughts were on the Olympic Games.

Jesse breaks the tape to win the 100-meter sprint during the semifinals at Princeton.

THE ROAD TO BERLIN

As 1936 arrived, the world looked forward to the Summer Olympics. The games began in ancient Greece over 2,500 years ago. After a long lapse they were revived in 1896 and were held every four years. They ranked as the supreme test for **amateur athletes**.

Olympic runners are not picked by how well they have run in the past. Jesse had to win his place on the U.S. team. That winter low grades kept him from running the indoor meets with the team. He was forced to train on his own. By spring his grades were better. Coach Snyder welcomed him back to the team.

To earn a trip to Berlin, Jesse had to win three major meets. His first stop was in Chicago. There he won the 100-meter and 200-meter sprints and the long jump. On July 4 Jesse ran in the semifinals at Princeton. Again he beat out the competition in his three events.

A week later the finals took place on Randall's Island, in New York City. A storm drenched the field early in the day, but Jesse kept his mind on business. Running smoothly and strongly he won both the 100-meter and the 200-meter events. Then he soared to a third win in the long jump. Mack Robinson made the team by coming in second in the 200. Jackie, Mack's younger brother, later became the first black to play major league baseball.

Jesse met the great Babe Ruth a few days later. "You gonna win at the Olympics?" the home run slugger asked.

Smiling, Jesse said he would try to win.

The Babe frowned. "Trying don't mean nothin'," he said. "I *know* I'm going to hit a home run just about every time I swing that bat. I'm surprised when I don't."

Jesse took the Babe's advice to heart. He saw that it was not enough to *want* to win. Now he added "Know you will win" to Coach Riley's "Run to beat yourself."

The SS *Manhattan* sailed for Germany on July 15. Jesse posed for pictures in his blue pinstripe suit. It was the only suit he owned. The coaches warned the athletes not to eat too much of the ship's good food. Jesse did not need the warning. He was seasick for most of the trip.

After nine long days the ship docked at Bremen. The team took a train to Berlin and moved into the Olympic Village. Jesse met athletes from all over the world. Rain fell each day as the runners and jumpers worked themselves back into shape.

In 1936 Jesse won four gold medals at the Berlin Olympics. Almost 50 years later another American runner equaled his feat. Who was the runner?

After watching Jesse's workouts, the American coaches tried to change his running style. Luckily Coach Snyder had paid his own way to Berlin. He told the coaches to leave Jesse alone. Snyder also found new track shoes after Jesse lost his best pair.

Jesse could not ignore the **Nazi** flags that hung from every public building. Adolf Hitler, the ruthless **dictator**, claimed that Germans were a master race. He said that Jews, blacks and other nonwhites were subhuman. Many Jews had already been thrown into **concentration camps**.

The German people did not seem to notice the color of Jesse's skin. They treated him like a hero. People begged for autographs and asked him to pose for pictures. Only Adolf Hitler and his Nazis turned their backs. Jesse smiled grimly and waited. His chance to show what a black man could do was coming.

 Jesse's feat of winning four gold medals in a single Olympics is no longer a record. Who holds the record, what is his sport, and how many medals did he win?

Jesse Owens wins the 100-meter dash in the 1936 Olympics in an amazing 10.3 seconds.

OLYMPIC GOLD

A huge crowd filled Olympic Stadium on August 1, 1936. Adolf Hitler took his place as the host of the Games. One by one the teams of 53 nations entered the stadium. Each dipped its flag in salute as the athletes marched past Hitler's box. Only the American team refused to salute the dictator in this way.

Sailors raised a huge Olympic flag. The flag's five rings stand for the five continents linked in the Olympic spirit. After groups of white doves were set free, a runner entered with the Olympic torch. The flame had been carried in relays all the way from Greece.

The first races were held on August 2. Sixty-eight runners were entered in the 100-meter dash. That meant Jesse had to win a series of **trial heats** to reach the finals. In his morning heat Jesse equaled the world record of 10.3 seconds. Later, with the wind behind him, he clipped a tenth of a second from his time. This record of 10.2 seconds was not recognized because of the wind.

The finals were held the next day on a muddy track. Jesse drew the inside lane for the finals. That was bad luck, because the inside lanes had been chewed up by other runners.

Jesse dug his **starting holes** into the cinder track. All the years of training had led him to this moment. As the starter raised his pistol Jesse stared at the finish line. The next ten seconds would test his body and mind as no other race had.

The huge crowd was on its feet as the gun cracked. Timing his start perfectly Jesse streaked down the track. Ralph Metcalfe moved up close behind him, but Jesse would not be denied. He broke the tape and won the race in 10.3 seconds.

Jesse Owens broad jumping in the 1936 Olympics

The crowd chanted his name as Jesse took his place on the winner's stand. He stood tall and straight as a band played the "Star-Spangled Banner." Jesse was given a laurel wreath, a gold medal and a tiny oak tree. In later years he said that the ceremony was the happiest moment of his life.

On the first day of racing Hitler had called two German winners to his box. When Jesse was not invited American papers reported that Hitler had snubbed the black runner. They failed to report that Olympics officials had told Hitler to greet all winners—or none. After the first day Hitler chose to greet no one.

August 4 was a busy day for Jesse. Early in the morning he won a spot in the 200-meter semifinals. Then he turned to the long jump pit. As usual he did a run-through in his sweat suit. To his surprise, that was counted as the first of his three jumps. Nervous now, he fouled on his second try. Luz Long, a German jumper, took Jesse aside. Luz told Jesse not to take any chances. Start your jump a foot behind the takeoff board, he advised. Jesse took the advice and qualified on his last try.

That afternoon Jesse and Luz battled for the gold medal. After two jumps the men were tied. On his last try Jesse promised himself he would stay in the air forever. He was almost as good as his word. When he came down he owned a new Olympic record of 26 feet, $5^5/_{16}$ inches. Luz could not match it. He and Jesse walked off the field with their arms around each other.

Jesse won fame as a track and field athlete. At one time, however, he was hired by the New York Mets baseball team. What was Jesse's job with the Mets?

27

A weary Jesse was back on the track the next day. In his first race he breezed into the 200-meter finals. That set the stage for the afternoon. Running in a drizzle, Jesse won his third gold medal. His time of 20.7 seconds set a world record for a 200-meter run around a curve.

The rain turned to a downpour as Jesse accepted his medal. Only the American coaches knew he had one more race to run.

NEW RACES TO RUN

With three gold medals in his pocket Jesse was ready to relax. The coaches had other ideas. They had heard that the Germans were saving their best sprinters for the 400-meter relay. A near-certain American victory now seemed in doubt.

The coaches called a meeting. They said they were dropping Marty Glickman and Sam Stoller from the team. Jesse and Metcalfe were named to replace them. Jesse spoke up. "I've won three gold medals," he said. "Let [Marty and Sam] run, they deserve it."

Glickman pointed out that he and Stoller were the team's only Jews. "If we don't run," he said, "it will be a victory for the Nazis." The coaches only shook their heads. They went ahead and picked Owens, Metcalfe, Draper and Wykoff for the team.

 When Jesse met with young athletes he often talked about the three Ds. "That's what helped make me an Olympic champion," he would say. What were Jesse's three Ds?

The 400-meter relay team of the 1936 Olympics

Jesse was angry, but it did not show in his running. He led off in fine style, passing the baton to Metcalfe with a five-yard lead. From there it was a runaway. The American team set a new world record of 39.8 seconds. The German "superteam" came in a distant third.

Jesse's four medals in track and field tied a record set in 1900. He was now a superstar. Big-money offers poured in. **Vaudeville** star Eddie Cantor offered him $40,000 for ten weeks' work. A dance band said it would pay him $25,000 to announce its songs.

Jesse Owens, Ohio State's Olympic hero, pictured with Mayor Harold H. Burton of Cleveland in the parade that marked Owens's return to Cleveland

"I'm anxious to finish my college career," Jesse said. "But I can't afford to miss this chance if it really means big money." Jesse decided to leave college and take advantage of these money making opportunities.

While the offers piled up, the **Amateur Athletic Union (AAU)** kept the team busy. Because the AAU was short of cash, officials booked meets all over Europe. The income went to pay the team's Olympic bills. No one seemed to notice that the athletes were worn out. The constant running caused Jesse to lose ten pounds.

At last Jesse and Coach Snyder announced they would not go on. When the team left for Sweden, Jesse sailed for home. The AAU quickly suspended him.

For the moment Jesse did not care. The great black singer and dancer Bill "Bojangles" Robinson met him at the dock in New York. The singer's manager, Marty Forkins, signed on as Jesse's agent. The city honored the new hero with a ticker tape parade.

Then, one by one, the offers vanished. The vaudeville deal was withdrawn. Movie studios and bandleaders changed their minds. As Jesse said, "Everyone was going to slap me on the back. . . but no one was going to offer me a job."

To add to his problems, the AAU declared that Jesse was now a pro. They did this because he had signed with an agent. As a pro he could no longer run for OSU. Jesse saw that he had a new race to run. He had to find a way to support his family.

Jesse prepares for his nightclub debut with Bill "Bojangles" Robinson.

With Marty Forkins's help Jesse found work here and there. He spoke at banquets and made radio broadcasts. He endorsed food and clothing products. By train and plane he crisscrossed the country. No job paid much, but the checks added up. Jesse bought a home for his parents and a new Buick for himself.

Jesse made more headlines when he agreed to support Alf Landon for president. The Republican party paid him $10,000 to speak from the back of a campaign train. After talking about the Olympics, Jesse always ended with a few good words for Landon.

The voters loved Jesse, but they refused to vote for his candidate. Landon lost in a landslide.

BUILDING A NEW LIFE

The AAU could keep Jesse from running as an amateur. It could not keep him from running. Now when Jesse ran, he did not run for medals. He ran for money.

In December of 1936 Jesse went to Cuba to race. The Cuban runner, under AAU pressure, withdrew at the last minute. A promoter then matched Jesse against a horse. With a 40-yard handicap, Jesse actually beat the horse. Jesse earned $2,000 for taking on this strange challenge.

How do experts explain the faster times and longer distances achieved by today's track and field stars?

Jesse outruns a horse.

Jesse's wife, Ruth, and his three daughters did not see Jesse very often. In 1937 he toured with a black band. He served as bandleader and sang a little. "I can't carry a tune in a bucket," he admitted later. After that gig Jesse went on the road with black basketball and softball teams. In addition, Jesse became a major investor in a dry cleaning firm. The teams lost money, as did his dry cleaning firm. The government came after him for not paying his taxes. By 1939 Jesse was bankrupt.

Jesse coaches a swimming class at a boys' club in Chicago.

At age 27 Jesse went back to college. To pay his way he helped coach the track team. It was a brave effort, but Jesse could not pass his math classes. Later in the fall of 1940 he left OSU a second time. A college degree was still out of reach.

Life took a new turn when the United States entered World War II. As head of a household Jesse could not be drafted. That did not keep him from aiding the war effort. At first he headed a national physical fitness program. Then a better job turned up at the Ford Motor Company. Ford was hiring thousands of black workers to build tanks and trucks. Jesse's job was to pick good workers for the assembly lines. He also did his best to improve housing and recreation for blacks.

When the war ended, Ford went back to making cars. Jesse lost his job along with thousands of others, but his name was still magic. People listened when he spoke. He moved to Chicago and plugged products on radio and, later, on television. As his client list grew, Jesse formed a public relations firm to deal with business matters. It was about this time that he began a 30-year smoking habit. He seemed to have forgotten how weak his lungs were when he was a boy.

Because of the war the Olympics were not held in 1940 and 1944. No one knows what records Jesse might have set at those lost games. In 1950, at age 37, he ran a 100-yard dash in 9.7 seconds. Sportswriters had not forgotten him. They picked Jesse as the greatest track athlete of the half century.

TRIVIA 10 Jesse's daughter Marlene won an honor at OSU that Jesse could not have won. What honor did Marlene win?

Jesse Owens meets with Richard Nixon during a campaign tour.

During the 1950s Jesse often traveled overseas for the State Department. In 1956 he was a popular stand-in for President Eisenhower at the Olympic Games in Australia. Jesse made friends wherever he went. *Life* magazine called him "a perfect envoy."

THE RACE COMES TO AN END

Time was catching up with Jesse. His daughters were growing up and he hardly knew them. His parents were dead. One by one his records fell to strong young runners. His 60-meter dash record was the last to fall. In 1978 Ruth talked him into moving to Arizona for the clear air of the Southwest. The move came too late. Jesse soon learned that he had lung cancer.

Doctors did their best, but Jesse lost his last race. He died on March 31, 1980, in Tucson, Arizona. The governor declared a day of mourning for the former world's fastest person.

Jesse Owens proves there's still plenty of spring in his legs as he hurdles a street barricade in a Chicago park in 1960.

Wearing his Olympic laurel wreath, Jesse Owens displays three of his four gold medals won in the 1936 Olympics.

Jesse Owens, Track Immortal

Track stars have brief careers. Like shooting stars they light up the sky for an instant—and then they are gone. Jesse Owens did not fit that pattern. His star still burns today.

Jesse earned his first headlines as a high school runner. A few years later he ran his way into the history books. His four Olympic medals made him the best-known runner in the history of sport.

After the Olympics Jesse worked hard to earn love as well as respect. As a black man he often felt the sting of racial abuse. Some blacks thought he should fight back, but Jesse did not think that way. He was not an angry man. "Work hard," he told blacks, "and doors will open for you." His own life, Jesse thought, could serve as an example.

Jesse Owens teams up with youthful fund-raisers to collect money to send the 1972 U.S. team to the Summer Olympic Games.

As he aged the nation took note of Jesse's public service. In 1972 OSU awarded him an honorary doctor of athletic arts degree. Jesse treasured that long-sought college diploma. Two years later he was named to the Track and Field Hall of Fame. Then the White House called. In 1976 President Ford gave Jesse the nation's highest civilian award—the Medal of Freedom. Three years later President Carter gave him the Living Legends Award. Jesse, Carter said, "inspired others to reach for greatness."

Jesse was at his best as a public speaker. Those who heard him said he could have been a great preacher. Jesse never wrote out his talks; he spoke from the heart. An old teammate said, "He emphasized God, mother, country, hard work and clean living." His warmth and good humor came across as he spoke. People liked him, even when they did not agree with his message.

Today Jesse lives on in memory. Ohio State University named a track complex for him. The Jesse Owens Foundation helps needy youths get to college. Sports awards, scholarships and track meets bear his name. In Berlin the street leading to the Olympic Stadium is named *Jesse Owens Strasse*. In 1990 Jesse became one of the few athletes pictured on a U.S. postage stamp.

Jesse died four years before the 1984 Olympic Games came to Los Angeles. He would have loved the tribute he was given there. On the opening day a young black woman carried the Olympic torch into the Coliseum. She was Gina Hemphill, Jesse's granddaughter. A giant screen showed film clips of the Berlin Olympics. Once again Jesse's flying feet barely seemed to touch the track.

Jesse Owens revisits the Olympic Stadium in the British sector of Berlin 15 years after his show of skill there in the 1936 Olympic Games.

SPEERWERFEN ~~~~~
DISKUSWERFEN WOELLKE D~~
KUGELSTOSSEN WOELLKE D~~
HAMMERWERFEN HEIN DEUTSCHL~~
ZEHNKAMPF MORRIS U.S.A.
LEICHTATHLETIK FRAU
100 m LAUF STEPHENS U.S.A.
80 m HÜRDENLAUF VALLA ITALIEN
HOCHSPRUNG CSAK UNGARN
DISKUSWERFEN MAUERMAYER DEUTSCHLAN~
SPEERWERFEN FLEISCHER DEUTSCHLAND
4 × 100 m STAFFELLAUF U.S.A.
MODERNER FÜNFKAM~
HANDRICK DEUTSCHLAND
SCHWIMMEN MÄNNE~
100 m FREISTIL CSIK UNGARN
100 m RÜCKENSTIL ~~~~~ U.S.A.
200 m BRUSTSTIL HAMURO JAPAN
400 m FREISTIL MEDICA U.S.A.
1500 m FREISTIL TERADA JAPAN
KUNSTSPRINGEN DEGENER U.S.A.
TURMSPRINGEN WAYNE U.S.A.
4 × 200 m STAFFEL JAPAN
WASSERBALLSPIEL UNGARN

Jesse Owens at the broad jumping event of the 1936 NCAA meet in Chicago

GLOSSARY

amateur athlete—Someone who competes for the love of the sport, not for money.

Amateur Athletic Union (AAU)—In the 1930s the AAU was the governing body for amateur sport in the United States. The AAU also controlled the selection of athletes for the U.S. Olympic team.

anchor—The athlete who runs the last leg in a relay race.

Big Ten—A nickname for the midwestern colleges that compete in the Big Ten Conference.

Buckeyes—The nickname of the OSU athletic teams. A buckeye is the nut produced by the buckeye tree.

concentration camps—Giant prisons where dictators lock up people who are thought to be threats to the state. Many inmates die of overwork, starvation, or in gas chambers.

dictator—A ruler who has absolute power over a country.

ghetto—A section of a city where many minority people live because of social, legal or economic pressure.

Great Depression—The time during the 1930s when the U.S. economy collapsed and many people lost their jobs.

Nazi—A member of Adolf Hitler's National Socialist political party, which was in control in Germany from 1933–1945.

pneumonia—A disease often caused by a virus, characterized by a severe inflammation of the lungs.

sharecroppers—Poor farmers who pay the rent on their farms by giving part of their crops to the landowner.

starting holes—Before starting blocks were invented, runners dug holes in the track to help them in their starts.

trial heats—Preliminary races held to determine who will be allowed to run in the finals of a big race.

vaudeville—A stage show made up of a series of short acts. A typical vaudeville show would feature singers, dancers, comedians, jugglers and magicians.

MORE GOOD READING ABOUT JESSE OWENS

Baker, William. *Jesse Owens: An American Life*. New York: The Free Press, 1986.

Bortstein, Larry. "Jesse Owens," in *After Olympic Glory: The Lives of Ten Outstanding Medalists*. New York: Frederick Warne, 1978.

Gentry, Tony. *Jesse Owens*. New York: Chelsea House Publishers, 1990.

Johnson, William. "A Professional Good Example," in *All That Glitters Is Not Gold*. New York: G. P. Putnam's Sons, 1972.

Mandell, Richard. "Jesse Owens," in *The Nazi Olympics*. New York: Macmillan Publishing Company, 1971.

Owens, Jesse, with Paul Neimark. *The Jesse Owens Story*. New York: G. P. Putnam's Sons, 1970.

Owens, Jesse with Paul Neimark. *Jesse: The Man Who Outran Hitler*. New York: Fawcett Gold Medal, 1978.

JESSE OWENS TRIVIA QUIZ

1: As a high school senior, Jesse set a new world record in the 220-yard dash. He tied the record in the 100-yard dash.

2: Jesse would have to improve in all four events to win medals in a modern Olympics:
   100-meter dash: Jesse Owens (1936), 10.3 sec.
Carl Lewis (U.S., 1988), 9.92 sec.
   200-meter dash: Jesse Owens (1936), 20.7 sec.
Joe DeLoach (U.S., 1988), 19.75 sec.
   Long jump: Jesse Owens (1936), 26 feet, 5$^5/_{16}$ in.
Bob Beamon (U.S., 1968), 29 feet, 2$^1/_2$ in.
   400-meter relay: Owens, Metcalfe, Draper, Wykoff (1936)—39.8 sec.
Graddy, Brown, Smith, Lewis (U.S., 1984)—37.83 sec.

3: Jesse gave two of the trees to his old schools—East Tech and OSU. He planted the third tree in his mother's backyard. The fourth tree died.

4: No. Luz Long later joined the German army and was killed during World War II. After the war Jesse visited Berlin and had an emotional reunion with Luz's son.

5: Carl Lewis equaled Jesse's feat at the 1984 Olympics in Los Angeles. Lewis won the same four events, beating Jesse's marks in each of them.

6: In 1972 American swimmer Mark Spitz won seven gold medals. Spitz won four individual races, swam on three winning relay teams—and set world records in all seven events.

7: In 1965 the Mets hired Jesse as an exercise and running coach. Jesse worked hard to get the team in shape, but the Mets still played badly that year.

8: Jesse's three Ds were determination, discipline and dedication. He knew that it takes strength of character as well as talent to become a champion.

9: Experts explain that today's athletes have the advantages of (1) more intense training methods, (2) improved techniques and equipment, (3) all-weather tracks and jumping pits and (4) tougher competition, all of which may increase the athletes' efforts.

10: In 1960 Marlene was elected Homecoming Queen at OSU. She was the first black woman to win that title.

Index

Amateur Athletic Union (AAU) 30, 31, 32
Ann Arbor, Michigan 5
Australia 36

Berlin, Germany 22, 23, 24, 40
Big Ten 5, 21
Bolton Elementary School 11

Cantor, Eddie 29
Carter, Jimmy 40
Chicago, Illinois 22, 35
Cleveland, Ohio 10, 12, 16, 18
Cuba 32

Draper, Foy 28

East Cleveland Technical High School 12, 14, 15
Eisenhower, Dwight D. 36
Europe 30
Evanston, Illinois 16

Fairmount Junior High School 12, 14, 15
Ford, Gerald 40
Ford Motor Company 35
Forkins, Marty 31, 32

Glickman, Marty 28
Great Depression 15
Greece 22, 25

Hemphill, Gina 40
Hitler, Adolf 24, 25, 27

Lake Erie 10
Landon, Alf 32
Life magazine 36
Living Legends Award 40
Long, Luz 27
Los Angeles, California 40

Medal of Freedom 40
Metcalfe, Ralph 16, 21, 26, 28, 29

National Interscholastic Meet 18
New York 21, 31

Oakville, Alabama 8, 9
Ohio State University (OSU) 5, 19, 31, 35, 40
Olympics 15, 16, 21, 22, 23, 25, 27, 30, 32, 35, 36, 39, 40
Owens, Emma 8, 10, 11, 12, 15, 16
Owens, Gloria 18
Owens, Henry 8, 9, 10, 11, 12, 15
Owens, Ruth Solomon 16, 18, 21, 34, 37

Peacock, Eulace 21
Princeton, New Jersey 22

Randall's Island, New York 23
Riley, Charles "Pop" 12, 13, 14, 15, 16, 19, 21, 23
Robinson, Bill "Bojangles" 31
Robinson, Jackie 23
Robinson, Mack 23
Ruth, Babe 23

Snyder, Larry 5, 19, 20, 21, 22, 24, 31
Stoller, Sam 28
Sweden 31

Track and Field Hall of Fame 40
Tucson, Arizona 37

United States (America) 11, 22, 25, 27, 28, 29, 35

White House 40
World War II 35
Wykoff, Frank 28

48